PARALLEL LIVES

FREDERICK DOUGLASS
Born in 1818
AMELIA BLOOMER

Julie Knutson

CHERRY LAKE PRESS

Published in the United States of America by Cherry Lake Publishing
Ann Arbor, Michigan
www.cherrylakepublishing.com

Reading Adviser: Marla Conn, MS, Ed., Literacy specialist, Read-Ability, Inc.
Cover Designer: Felicia Macheske

Photo Credits: © National Archives/Frank W. Legg photographic collection of portraits of nineteenth-century notables, 1862–1884/Identifier 558770, cover, 1 [left]; © Science History Images/Alamy Stock Photo, cover, 2 [right]; © ZU_09/iStock.com, 5; © Library of Congress, LC-USZ62-100288, 6; © Library of Congress, LC-DIG-highsm-09902, 9; ©pixelheadphoto/iStock.com, 10; © Everett Historical/Shutterstock.com, 12, 26; © Dmitriy_Danilov/Shutterstock.com, 15; © Library of Congress, LC-USZ62-15887, 16; © Marzolino/Shutterstock.com, 19; © Courtesy of National Archives, 21; © Courtesy of National Portrait Gallery, 22; © Library of Congress, 24; © Library of Congress, 25

Library of Congress Cataloging-in-Publication Data

Names: Knutson, Julie, author.
Title: Born in 1818 : Frederick Douglass and Amelia Bloomer / by Julie Knutson.
Description: Ann Arbor, Michigan : Cherry Lake Publishing, [2020] | Series: Parallel lives | Includes bibliographical references and index. | Audience: Grades 4-6
Identifiers: LCCN 2019033447 (print) | LCCN 2019033448 (ebook) | ISBN 9781534159150 (hardcover) | ISBN 9781534161450 (paperback) | ISBN 9781534160309 (pdf) | ISBN 9781534162600 (ebook)
Subjects: LCSH: Douglass, Frederick, 1818-1895—Juvenile literature. | Abolitionists—United States—Biography—Juvenile literature. | Bloomer, Amelia Jenks, 1818-1894—Juvenile literature. | Feminists—United States—Biography—Juvenile literature. | Women's rights—United States—Juvenile literature.
Classification: LCC E449.D75 K58 2020 (print) | LCC E449.D75 (ebook) | DDC 973.8092 [B]—dc23
LC record available at https://lccn.loc.gov/2019033447
LC ebook record available at https://lccn.loc.gov/2019033448

Cherry Lake Publishing would like to acknowledge the work of the Partnership for 21st Century Learning, a Network of Battelle for Kids. Please visit www.battelleforkids.org/networks/p21 for more information.

Printed in the United States of America
Corporate Graphics

ABOUT THE AUTHOR

Julie Knutson shares a birth year with Venus Williams, Chelsea Clinton, and Lin-Manuel Miranda. An avid student of history and former teacher, she lives in northern Illinois with her husband and son.

TABLE OF CONTENTS

CHAPTER 1

Welcome to 1818

1818. Social reformers Frederick Douglass and Amelia Bloomer are born into an America in which **injustice**, **discrimination**, and **inequality** are not just legal, but a normal part of everyday life. Frederick and Amelia both used written and spoken word to try to change this, spreading the message that all people should have equal rights under the law.

Abolitionism: By 1818, slavery had a nearly 200-year history in America. As new ideas about human rights spread during the late 1700s, people began to question the morality of slavery. How could a country, founded on liberty and justice, allow millions of

Slavery did not end in the United States until 1865.

In the 19th century, women rarely received a formal education.

people to be enslaved? **Abolitionists** argued for an end to slavery. The cause gained significant momentum in the early 19th century and was a well-organized movement by 1818.

Women's Issues: In the early 19th century, middle- and upper-middle class white women were expected to manage their households and not participate in public life. While poor and enslaved women might work outside of the home, their wages weren't theirs to keep. Politics and business were considered a man's domain. Women couldn't own land, collect their own income, inherit money, or vote. They were considered the property of their husbands or fathers.

The "Separate Spheres"

In the 19th century, women and men were expected to live in "separate ***spheres****." A woman's proper place was considered the home, or* ***domestic*** *sphere, while a man's place was the broader world.*

CHAPTER 2

Frederick Douglass (b. 1818)

For slaves who'd escaped to free states in the North, the simple act of speaking out could endanger their lives. If captured, they could be sent back to their legal owners. But this didn't stop Frederick Douglass. For Frederick, the truth needed to be told, because *his* truth exposed the brutality of slavery. For more than half a century, Frederick risked his life to fight for black civil rights by speaking, writing, and acting in support of justice.

Early Years: Finding a Voice

Exactly *when* Frederick was born remains a mystery. Born into slavery in Talbot County, Maryland, Frederick spent his earliest years in the care of his grandparents. He met his mother a total of four or five times, and never knew his father. Young Frederick had

Frederick Douglass famously said, "If there is no struggle, there is no progress." This quote continues to inspire activists today.

Frederick Douglass was determined to learn to read. He traded bread on the street with hungry children for lessons.

little control over the *who, what,* and *where* of his existence. Around age 6, his grandmother was sold away to another plantation. At age 9, he was sent to live with the family of slave owner Hugh Auld in Baltimore, Maryland.

While living with the Aulds, Frederick began developing a key skill: reading. Sophia Auld, Hugh's wife, taught Frederick alongside her own son. When Hugh found out about Sophia's lessons, he was furious. He told his wife that "teaching a slave to read will make him unfit to be a slave." Frederick made a key connection at this moment between literacy and slavery: in reading—and learning—lay the promise of **emancipation**. He kept reading whatever he could, whenever and wherever he could find it. This wasn't an easy task. Enslaved people couldn't go to school or possess books. There were no formal opportunities to practice. But Frederick was determined to learn.

Like many enslaved people, Frederick was passed from household to plantation and owner to owner. In his late teens, he was hired out as a laborer in Baltimore's shipyards. There, he met free black sailors who enjoyed the freedom he'd only dared dream of. Now, he saw that this freedom could be a reality.

At 19, he met and fell in love with a free black woman named Anna Murray. Frederick and Anna wanted a life together, in freedom. They hatched a plan for his escape. He would borrow the papers of a free sailor friend, and Anna would make him a uniform to match this identity. Then, he would attempt to flee to New York. The plan worked. On September 3, 1838, Frederick escaped. A few weeks later, Anna joined him, and the couple was married.

It was dangerous for Frederick to publish his autobiography. At any moment he could have been captured and sent back.

Middle Years: Expressing a Voice

Frederick and Anna settled in New Bedford, Massachusetts, a city with an active abolitionist community. Frederick attended local anti-slavery meetings, and began sharing his own life story as a way of speaking out against slavery. Crowds assembled and listened. Frederick the **orator** was born. He toured America—and eventually England and Ireland—telling his story to all who would listen and arguing for the end of slavery. He wasn't always warmly received. In Indiana, he was beaten and his hands were broken. Hostile crowds threw bricks, eggs, and vegetables. But Frederick spoke on.

Frederick didn't stop with the spoken word. He also set his story to paper. *The Narrative of the Life of Frederick Douglass* was first published in 1845. An immediate sensation, the book offered an account of Frederick's life from birth to separation from his

Douglass and John Brown

In 1859, abolitionist John Brown hatched a plan to attack the federal **arsenal** *at Harpers Ferry. John's plan was to raid the storehouse for weapons and redistribute them to enslaved people, who would use them to fight for freedom. John and Frederick Douglass were friends who frequently corresponded. While Frederick tried to convince John that the raid would not work, John proceeded. Many of his fellow raiders were killed, and John was captured. A letter from Frederick was found with John's belongings. Fearful that he would be linked to the plan, Frederick fled first to Canada and then to England. John was hanged on December 2, 1859.*

family to life in New Bedford. It was reprinted 9 times over the next 3 years. Slave narratives such as Frederick's were a powerful tool in building **empathy**, allowing people far and wide to hear his story and imagine the horrors of slavery. Throughout his career, he founded newspapers and publications to inform, connect, and empower readers to the causes of abolitionism and **suffrage**.

The North Star

Frederick Douglass began publishing his first abolitionist newspaper, The North Star, *in 1847. The publication was named after the night sky marker that enslaved people followed on their journey to freedom. The newspaper's motto was "Right is of no Sex – Truth is of no Color – God is the Father of us all, and we are all brethren." This showed his interest in the shared causes of racial and gender equality.*

The North Star is one of the brightest stars in the sky. This made it easy for slaves seeking freedom in Northern states to follow it.

Among his many accomplishments, Frederick is also the most photographed man of the 19th century.

Frederick also used his voice to influence policy. During the Civil War, he criticized President Lincoln's policy of excluding black soldiers from the Union army. After the bloody battle of Gettysburg in 1863, Lincoln changed course and allowed black soldiers to enlist. Over 180,000 black men—many of whom were formerly enslaved—took up arms for the Union cause. When these soldiers were denied equal pay and the possibility of advancement in rank, Frederick got involved again. He never stopped in his pursuit of fairness and justice, even in discussions with the highest-ranking officials in the land.

Later Years: Leaving a Legacy

In 1865, Frederick Douglass saw slavery abolished with the passage of the 13th Amendment to the U.S. Constitution. In the coming years, the 14th and 15th Amendments were passed, which gave citizenship to all people born or **naturalized** in the United States and granted black men the right to vote. These amendments transformed America into a significantly different country than the one Frederick was born into in 1818. Frederick's willingness to tell his story and argue against slavery were critical in bringing about these changes.

CHAPTER 3

Amelia Bloomer (b. May 27, 1818)

In 1851, the name "Bloomer" became **synonymous** with a revolutionary fashion development: a comfortable pair of loose-fitting pants worn with a short skirt over top. The garment got its name from journalist and social reformer Amelia Bloomer, who advocated for a wide range of causes throughout the second half of the 19th century. On topics ranging from **temperance** to suffrage to clothing reform, Amelia had something to say. She used her newspaper to speak on these topics. *The Lily* was the world's first newspaper solely dedicated to and edited by women.

Women's dresses at the time could weigh upwards of 15 pounds (6.8 kilograms)!

Early Years: Finding a Voice

By her own account, Amelia's early life was ordinary. Born and raised in Homer, New York, Amelia had little formal schooling. Nevertheless, she worked as a teacher and later as a **governess**. While employed as a governess in Seneca Falls, New York, she met Dexter Bloomer. The pair soon married. A law student and newspaper editor, Dexter encouraged his new wife to write. Writing became a way for Amelia to explore her thoughts and share them with the world.

Amelia wrote for *The Seneca County Courier.* At the same time, she got involved in a variety of civic and social causes in Seneca Falls. She met other activists there working on other issues as well. A turning point in women's history was the Seneca Falls Convention of 1848. Attending it allowed her to experience firsthand the arguments for suffrage and full political rights for women. It left her with a lot to think about. The following year, she took the next step in exercising her voice on temperance, women's issues, and social reform: she started her newspaper.

What happened at the Seneca Falls Convention?

In July 1848, the Seneca Falls Convention launched the movement to achieve equal rights for women. On its opening day, organizer Elizabeth Cady Stanton summarized its purpose in a list of **grievances***. These were later presented in a document called the Declaration of Sentiments, modeled on the Declaration of Independence. It that stated that women and men should enjoy equal rights in all areas, including politics, education, and jobs. The Declaration was signed by 68 women and 32 men, including Frederick Douglass, the only African American in attendance.*

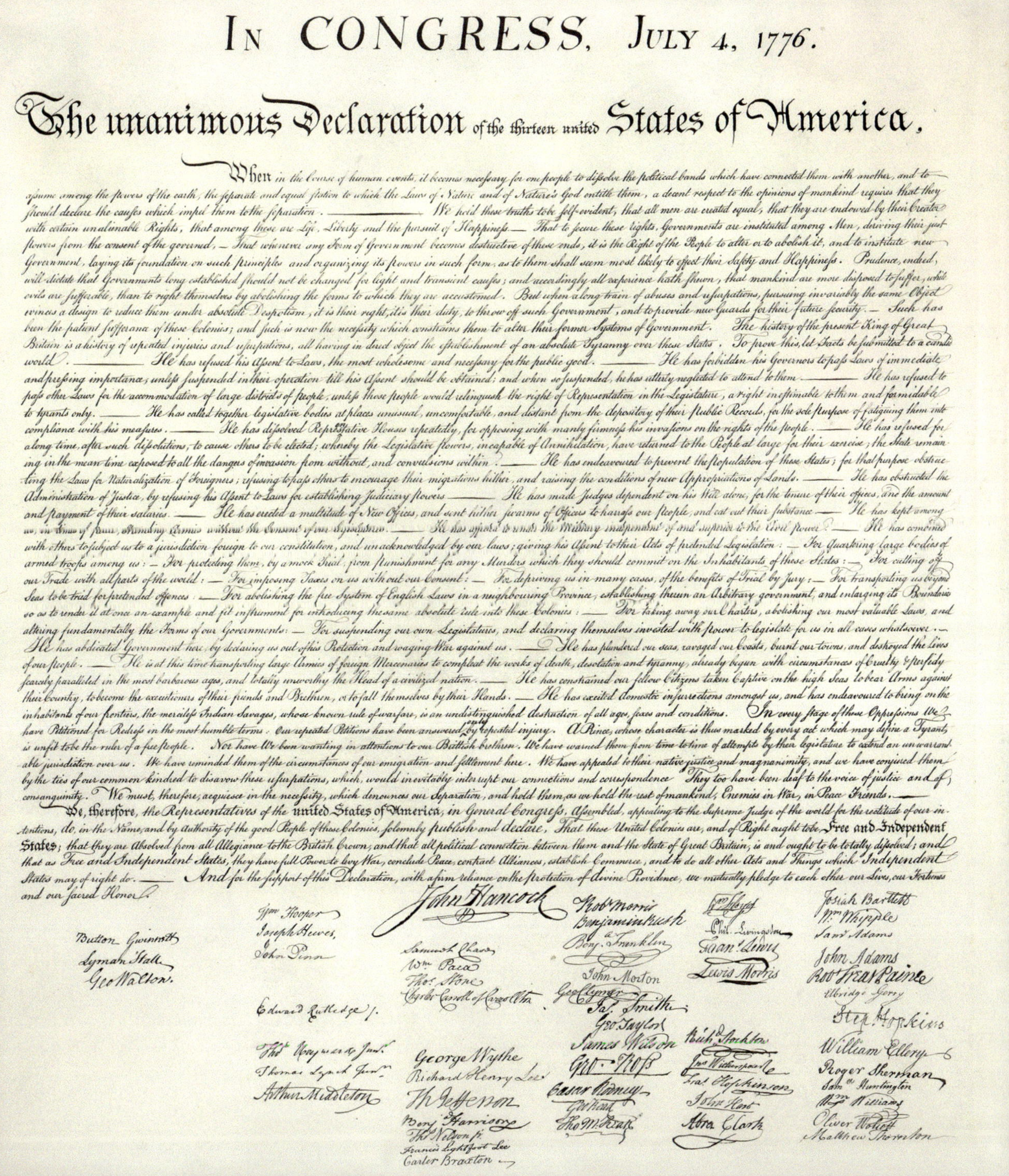
IN CONGRESS, JULY 4, 1776.

The unanimous Declaration of the thirteen united States of America,

When in the Course of human events, it becomes necessary for one people to dissolve the political bands which have connected them with another, and to assume among the powers of the earth, the separate and equal station to which the Laws of Nature and of Nature's God entitle them, a decent respect to the opinions of mankind requires that they should declare the causes which impel them to the separation. — We hold these truths to be self-evident, that all men are created equal, that they are endowed by their Creator with certain unalienable Rights, that among these are Life, Liberty and the pursuit of Happiness. — That to secure these rights, Governments are instituted among Men, deriving their just powers from the consent of the governed, — That whenever any Form of Government becomes destructive of these ends, it is the Right of the People to alter or to abolish it, and to institute new Government, laying its foundation on such principles and organizing its powers in such form, as to them shall seem most likely to effect their Safety and Happiness. Prudence, indeed, will dictate that Governments long established should not be changed for light and transient causes; and accordingly all experience hath shewn, that mankind are more disposed to suffer, while evils are sufferable, than to right themselves by abolishing the forms to which they are accustomed. But when a long train of abuses and usurpations, pursuing invariably the same Object evinces a design to reduce them under absolute Despotism, it is their right, it is their duty, to throw off such Government, and to provide new Guards for their future security. — Such has been the patient sufferance of these Colonies; and such is now the necessity which constrains them to alter their former Systems of Government. The history of the present King of Great Britain is a history of repeated injuries and usurpations, all having in direct object the establishment of an absolute Tyranny over these States. To prove this, let Facts be submitted to a candid world. — He has refused his Assent to Laws, the most wholesome and necessary for the public good. — He has forbidden his Governors to pass Laws of immediate and pressing importance, unless suspended in their operation till his Assent should be obtained; and when so suspended, he has utterly neglected to attend to them. — He has refused to pass other Laws for the accommodation of large districts of people, unless those people would relinquish the right of Representation in the Legislature, a right inestimable to them and formidable to tyrants only. — He has called together legislative bodies at places unusual, uncomfortable, and distant from the depository of their public Records, for the sole purpose of fatiguing them into compliance with his measures. — He has dissolved Representative Houses repeatedly, for opposing with manly firmness his invasions on the rights of the people. — He has refused for a long time, after such dissolutions, to cause others to be elected; whereby the Legislative powers, incapable of Annihilation, have returned to the People at large for their exercise; the State remaining in the mean time exposed to all the dangers of invasion from without, and convulsions within. — He has endeavoured to prevent the population of these States; for that purpose obstructing the Laws for Naturalization of Foreigners; refusing to pass others to encourage their migrations hither, and raising the conditions of new Appropriations of Lands. — He has obstructed the Administration of Justice, by refusing his Assent to Laws for establishing Judiciary powers. — He has made Judges dependent on his Will alone, for the tenure of their offices, and the amount and payment of their salaries. — He has erected a multitude of New Offices, and sent hither swarms of Officers to harrass our people, and eat out their substance. — He has kept among us, in times of peace, Standing Armies without the Consent of our legislatures. — He has affected to render the Military independent of and superior to the Civil power. — He has combined with others to subject us to a jurisdiction foreign to our constitution, and unacknowledged by our laws; giving his Assent to their Acts of pretended Legislation: — For Quartering large bodies of armed troops among us: — For protecting them, by a mock Trial, from punishment for any Murders which they should commit on the Inhabitants of these States: — For cutting off our Trade with all parts of the world: — For imposing Taxes on us without our Consent: — For depriving us in many cases, of the benefits of Trial by Jury: — For transporting us beyond Seas to be tried for pretended offences — For abolishing the free System of English Laws in a neighbouring Province, establishing therein an Arbitrary government, and enlarging its Boundaries so as to render it at once an example and fit instrument for introducing the same absolute rule into these Colonies: — For taking away our Charters, abolishing our most valuable Laws, and altering fundamentally the Forms of our Governments: — For suspending our own Legislatures, and declaring themselves invested with power to legislate for us in all cases whatsoever. — He has abdicated Government here, by declaring us out of his Protection and waging War against us. — He has plundered our seas, ravaged our Coasts, burnt our towns, and destroyed the lives of our people. — He is at this time transporting large Armies of foreign Mercenaries to compleat the works of death, desolation and tyranny, already begun with circumstances of Cruelty & perfidy scarcely paralleled in the most barbarous ages, and totally unworthy the Head of a civilized nation. — He has constrained our fellow Citizens taken Captive on the high Seas to bear Arms against their Country, to become the executioners of their friends and Brethren, or to fall themselves by their Hands. — He has excited domestic insurrections amongst us, and has endeavoured to bring on the inhabitants of our frontiers, the merciless Indian Savages, whose known rule of warfare, is an undistinguished destruction of all ages, sexes and conditions. In every stage of these Oppressions We have Petitioned for Redress in the most humble terms: Our repeated Petitions have been answered only by repeated injury. A Prince, whose character is thus marked by every act which may define a Tyrant, is unfit to be the ruler of a free people. Nor have We been wanting in attentions to our Brittish brethren. We have warned them from time to time of attempts by their legislature to extend an unwarrantable jurisdiction over us. We have reminded them of the circumstances of our emigration and settlement here. We have appealed to their native justice and magnanimity, and we have conjured them by the ties of our common kindred to disavow these usurpations, which, would inevitably interrupt our connections and correspondence. They too have been deaf to the voice of justice and of consanguinity. We must, therefore, acquiesce in the necessity, which denounces our Separation, and hold them, as we hold the rest of mankind, Enemies in War, in Peace Friends. —

We, therefore, the Representatives of the united States of America, in General Congress, Assembled, appealing to the Supreme Judge of the world for the rectitude of our intentions, do, in the Name, and by Authority of the good People of these Colonies, solemnly publish and declare, That these United Colonies are, and of Right ought to be Free and Independent States; that they are Absolved from all Allegiance to the British Crown, and that all political connection between them and the State of Great Britain, is and ought to be totally dissolved; and that as Free and Independent States, they have full Power to levy War, conclude Peace, contract Alliances, establish Commerce, and to do all other Acts and Things which Independent States may of right do. — And for the support of this Declaration, with a firm reliance on the protection of divine Providence, we mutually pledge to each other our Lives, our Fortunes and our sacred Honor.

John Hancock

Button Gwinnett, Lyman Hall, Geo Walton.

Wm Hooper, Joseph Hewes, John Penn

Edward Rutledge, Thos Heyward Junr., Thomas Lynch Junr., Arthur Middleton

Samuel Chase, Wm Paca, Thos Stone, Charles Carroll of Carrollton

George Wythe, Richard Henry Lee, Th Jefferson, Benja Harrison, Thos Nelson jr., Francis Lightfoot Lee, Carter Braxton

Robt Morris, Benjamin Rush, Benja Franklin, John Morton, Geo Clymer, Jas Smith, Geo Taylor, James Wilson, Geo Ross

Caesar Rodney, Geo Read, Tho M:Kean

Wm Floyd, Phil. Livingston, Frans Lewis, Lewis Morris

Richd Stockton, Jno Witherspoon, Fras Hopkinson, John Hart, Abra Clark

Josiah Bartlett, Wm Whipple, Saml Adams, John Adams, Robt Treat Paine, Elbridge Gerry

Step Hopkins, William Ellery

Roger Sherman, Samel Huntington, Wm Williams, Oliver Wolcott, Matthew Thornton

With 100 signatures, the Declaration of Sentiments has more signatures than the Declaration of Independence, which only had 56.

Elizabeth Cady Stanton wrote articles for *The Lily*.
She signed them using the pen name "Sunflower."

Middle Years: Expressing a Voice

In 1849, Amelia launched *The Lily*. While Dexter had encouraged her earlier writing aspirations, he wasn't so keen on this venture. Amelia and other women in Seneca Falls were determined. The publication wasn't **radical** in the beginning. It started as a way to insert women's voices into debates about temperance. But as it evolved, women's issues became more and more central. Contributors like Elizabeth Cady Stanton offered a closer look at suffrage and rights issues. The shift can also be seen in the paper's **masthead**, which was changed from "Devoted to the Interests of Women" in 1850 to, "(Dedicated to the) Emancipation of Women from Intemperance, Injustice, Prejudice, and Bigotry" in 1852.

In a February 1851 article, Amelia described a new fashion worn around town by her friend Elizabeth Smith Miller. Smith Miller ditched her rib-crushing **corset** and dirt-catching skirt for something new: pants with a short skirt over top. Previously, women had worn these types of outfits in health resorts. But Elizabeth wore them in public. Inspired to try out this look, Amelia made herself a pair and then wrote about it. She commented that the garment carried health benefits and allowed for free movement—and that it liberated women from the "**tyranny** of fashion."

The article didn't go unnoticed. As described in Dexter Bloomer's later book *The Life and Writings of Amelia Bloomer,* "Some praised and some blamed, some commented, and some ridiculed and condemned." In the summer of 1851, the praise

Feminism is often referred to in three waves. The first wave took place during the 19th century and focused mainly on the right to vote.

turned into a craze: there were bloomer balls and bloomer picnics. In textile factories in Lowell, Massachusetts, managers gave a banquet for women laborers who adopted the new style because they thought it safer for workers. However, Amelia and her allies who advocated for the style soon found it to be a distraction from other issues. In their view, people were focusing more on clothing than on more important issues like suffrage and the right to property and divorce.

Bloomers were popular because they offered women comfort and the ability to move around easily.

The 19th Amendment to the U.S. Constitution was passed in 1920. It granted women the right to vote.

Later Years: Leaving a Legacy

In 1854, Amelia and Dexter moved west, eventually settling in Iowa. She continued to work for suffrage for the rest of her life, serving as president of the Iowa Suffrage Association from 1871 to 1873. She also worked on behalf of Civil War soldiers and continued to lobby for temperance. Shortly before her 1894 death, bloomers came back into fashion. In 1893, many were touting the benefits of exercise, and women were taking to bicycles. Bloomers were suddenly both practical and fashionable.

Despite the times in which she lived, Amelia created spaces to speak and write about the issues that mattered most to her. Her efforts are still celebrated today. In 2017, the *Washington Post* launched its own version of *The Lily*, focusing on issues affecting modern women. Also, the American Library Association publishes an annual "Amelia Bloomer List" of notable feminist books for young readers.

Bike-Crazed and Bloomer-Clad

In 1894, Annie "Londonderry" Cohen Kopchovsky became the first woman to cycle around the world. She credited the feat—which would have been impossible in a long skirt and corset—to the bloomers she wore along the journey.

1818
Frederick is born in Talbot County, Maryland.

May 27, 1818
Amelia is born in Homer, New York.

1826
Frederick is sent to live with the Aulds in Baltimore, Maryland, and begins to learn to read.

1837
Frederick meets Anna Murray, his future wife.

September 1838
Frederick escapes to the North; Frederick and Anna marry.

1840
Amelia marries Dexter Bloomer.

1841
Frederick begins lecturing with abolitionist groups.

1845
The Narrative of the Life of Frederick Douglass is published.

1847
Frederick begins publishing the anti-slavery newspaper, *The North Star.*

July 1848
Frederick and Amelia attend the Seneca Falls Convention.

1849
Amelia begins publishing *The Lily*.

February 1851
Amelia pens an article that launches the "bloomers" craze.

1854
Amelia sells *The Lily*.

1863
Frederick convinces Lincoln to allow black soldiers to fight in the Union army. He recruits soldiers for the cause.

1865–1895
Frederick holds various appointed posts with the U.S. government.

1871–1873
Amelia serves as president of the Iowa Suffrage Association.

1894
Amelia passes away at age 76.

1895
Frederick dies at age 77.

1848 1850 1860 1870 1890

Research and Act

Writing was a key way both Frederick and Amelia shared their experiences, thoughts, passions, and concerns.

Research

What issue do you care about most? Whether it's animal welfare, the environment, school dress codes, homelessness, or other concerns, learn more about the topic. Read up on it. Learn how it became an issue, what challenges it poses, and what can be done about it.

Act

Think like Frederick and Amelia! Write an editorial for your school or local newspaper, sharing what you think can and should be done to address the problem you have researched.

Further Reading

Bloomer, Dexter C., ed. *Life and Writings of Amelia Bloomer.* Boston, MA: Arena Publishing Company, 1895. archive.org/details/lifeandwritings o028876mbp/page/n263

Bolden, Tonya. *Facing Frederick: The Life of Frederick Douglass, a Monumental American Man*. New York, NY: Abrams Books for Young Readers, 2017.

Harris, Duchess. *Women's Suffrage*. Minneapolis, MN: ABDO Publishing, 2018.

Morretta, Alison. *Frederick Douglass and William Garrison: A Partnership for Abolition*. New York, NY: Cavendish Square Publishing, 2016.

Prince, April Jones. *Who Was Frederick Douglass?* New York, NY: Grosset & Dunlap, 2014.

GLOSSARY

abolitionists (ab-uh-LISH-uh-nists) people who worked to put an end to slavery

arsenal (AHR-suh-nuhl) place where weapons are stored

corset (KOR-sit) clothing worn close to the skin, underneath other clothes to shape a woman's upper body

discrimination (dis-krim-ih-NAY-shuhn) unfair behavior to others based on differences in race or gender

domestic (duh-MES-tik) having to do with the home

emancipation (ih-man-suh-PAY-shuhn) freedom

empathy (EM-puh-thee) understanding how someone else feels

governess (GUHV-ur-nes) a woman who takes care of someone else's children in their home

grievances (GREE-vuhns-iz) things that are wrong and make you mad

inequality (in-ih-KWAH-lih-tee) differences that seem unfair between people or things

injustice (in-JUHS-tis) an unfair situation or action

masthead (MAST-hed) name of a newspaper or publication displayed at the top of the first page

naturalized (NACH-ur-uh-lized) made a citizen of a country that is different from the one the person was born in

orator (OR-uh-tur) public speaker

radical (RAD-ih-kuhl) in favor of extreme change in thinking

spheres (SFEERZ) areas of activity, interest, or knowledge

suffrage (SUHF-rij) right to vote

synonymous (sih-NAH-nuh-muhs) meaning the same thing

temperance (TEM-pruhns) a movement to ban alcohol consumption

tyranny (TIR-uh-nee) power that causes heavy burden on others

INDEX